57 STEPS
TO WALK INTO
GREATNESS

57 STEPS
TO WALK INTO
GREATNESS

Johnwext Preccio

authorHOUSE®

AuthorHouse™ LLC
1663 Liberty Drive
Bloomington, IN 47403
www.authorhouse.com
Phone: 1-800-839-8640

Published by AuthorHouse 12/20/2013

ISBN: 978-1-4918-3559-3 (sc)
ISBN: 978-1-4918-3558-6 (e)

DEDICATION

To
My ever-loving Mother ***Mrs. Phyllomyna Oghagbon Osa***

And
My Little Angel; ***Ovbiye Wealth Johnwext-Preccio***

CONTENTS

PROLOGUE

Courage is that virtue which champions the cause of right.
      __Cicero (De officiis)

It's better to die on your feet than live on your knees.
     __La passionaria (speech of Paris 1936)

Our doubts are traitors. And make us lose the good we oft might win, by fearing to attempt.
     __Shakespeare (Measure for measure)

Everyone is the architect of his (own) fortune.
     __Claudius Appius Caecus

Talent is a special gift from heaven; it's only persistent practice and devotion that can sustain its lifespan.
     __Johnwext Preccio

Ignorance is the night of the mind, a night without moon or star.
     __Confucius (Analects)

Change is the law of life, and those who look into the past and the present are certain to miss the future.
     __J.F. Kennedy

It's not the strongest of the species that survives, nor the most intelligent, but the most responsive to change.
     __Charles Darwin

If you have knowledge, let others light their candle at it.
　　　　　　　　　　__Magarett Fuller

Do not pray God to lower your mountains, pray he gives you the courage and strength to climb them to the top.
　　　　　　　　　　__Johnwext Preccio

ACKNOWLEDEGMENT

Let me start by saying a very big 'thank you' to God, the giver of wisdom, knowledge and understanding of these few lines of ideas that became a guide to people's success. Once more, God, I say; may your light keep shining in our lives as you become the strength of the weak, developer of every positive concept, the solid rock that never trembles.

More so, my parents are indispensable, for their love, patience and prayers, and I will not be pardoned if I forget to eulogize the one woman that stood out in the crowd, the strength of my bones, my encourager, and my source of focus—Mrs. Katheryne Johnwext Preccio (My invaluable wife).

My uncle, Engr. Judeson Osa, PhD., Dr. Benjamin O. Uhunmwangho; friends and well wishers who are too numerous to mention—May God richly bless you all.

And finally, Jake Elsen and Geraldine Bavastok (both of AuthorHouse publishers USA.), you guys were wonderfully indispensible.

FOREWORD

Because every change comes with a new pain, and it's obvious that those who refuse to change would continue to be bound in chains. Defy the dogmas of conventional approach of dealing with situations or circumstances; pull yourself together and take the bull by the horns. According to president Barrack Obama of the U.S.A., as part of his speech to eulogize the Americans and the world at large, for celebrating his victory with him on his swearing-in-day (January 20th 2009); he said and I quote, *"Whenever you fall, hop yourself up, dust yourself and forge ahead . . . indeed, you will excel".*

Walking into greatness is neither a fire-brigade pattern, nor a do-it-quick syndrome; but it's a peregrination that must be approached with utmost sense of seriousness, dexterity and the etiquette of success view point.

Make hay while the sun shines, try cutting the Gordian knot, abstain from chasing shadows instead of substances—do not forget; *all that glitters is not gold.* Do not let every *Tom, Dick or Harry* throw dust into your eyes, due to ignorance etc; *keep an eye on,* **even *when you are on the horns of a dilemma;*** do not be blindfolded by rejection or obsessed with the spirit of failures or confusion;—push on, the eleventh hour promises to come off with flying colours.

Your greatness is not to be negotiated; neither is it displayed at the market place for sale, so do not go a-begging due to the fear of losing out. Be bold to take your destiny in your own hands. You are God's best—do not subscribe to quitting, because God can't fail, you are a candidate of greatness not by virtue of power, but by the spirit of positive conviction that dwells inside of you.

1

SET A GOAL

Goals are like plans to houses, when they are not well drawn or the builders are not qualified to read the plan(s) they might end up not building the drawn plan thereby veering from the intended drawn house into something else etc.

As a matter of fact, two things could mar the realization of a goal; firstly, either the goal is too difficult to reach, which may daunt us, then we might give up on it; and

Secondly, the environment could also affect the process of reaching the summit; whereby for example, the goal required sufficient rainfall to fulfill the mission of the goal. When there's invariably no rain or low rainfall, it means the mission is to be aborted or carried forward etc.

In all, when the set goal seems too impossible to be actualized, it's safer and better to divide the goals into achievable units.

2

WORK OUT YOUR STRENGTH

America's invasion of Japan (Hiroshima and Nagasaki) in August, 1945, wasn't a mere war between a super-war-giant, full of trained war soldiers and dozens of sophisticated atomic weapons from underground submarines to jet bombers; and a less prepared nation (Japan) that was taken by surprise.

As a matter of fact, America didn't wake up one fateful morning and concluded they must come face-to-face with Japan, rather she must have planned her days, run research programs, drew their tactical plans etc on how to take the Japanese by surprise.

Your strengths are your knowledge, **knowledge is powerful**—*the exuberance of a youth is his strength and vigor, while that of the old ages is their grey hair.* So you had better define your prowess in order to defend your goal(s). More so, the Americans knew the only way to defend their superiority was to attack Japan cities of Hiroshima & Nagasaki [by taking them unawares].

Your strength is your skill and your skills come from learning, and learning by practicing; which in turn gives birth to perfection.

3

EVALUATE YOUR PASTS

People often say our pasts are often mirrored in our presents; thereby affecting our future a great deal.—In most cases, it either builds the courage of our success or breaks the defense of our breakthrough; wherefore we are left with no choice than failure.

Evaluation in other words, means accessing our past events, results etc. to score our outcomes, according to our deeds of either to score (rate) us above-or-below boards. Indeed, evaluation helps us in two ways; firstly, *if we are above boards, it encourages us to keep up the excellent deeds,* **and secondly,** *where we find faults in our actions or reactions, it's advisable to tighten our belt in order to sit where we desire by amending our ways.*

4

PAY FOR EVERYTHING

Most of us dread hardship as if it dictates the pace of our lifting; and many of us wish to have everything for free (without cost); but I must tell you, *in everything you get, you lose something in exchange;* such as, if you get something very treasured and attracted no bill; you had better be careful, either it's a trap or it's not worth what you think it's. As a matter of importance, *good things are not always cheap neither are cheap things usually good.*

Indeed, paying for every service one gets, puts one ahead of every condition that could have threatened the progress of outcomes—such conditions as delay, shortcomings etc. Moreover, the more you keep paying, the more you will feel challenged; and once you are challenged you will strive to get the work done.

5

SAVE TIME

Nothing annoys a Time Custodian than avoidable and deliberate waste of precious *"time"*. Moreover, because time is very essential in everything worth doing well, we can't afford to let it come to ruin by either human or other living things as the case may be.

More so, *"time"* is a veritable tool for success and if one must succeed, he needs to be a good friend of time. As a matter of fact, Time, being an invaluable asset in the choice of making enviable success in our generation and beyond.

Time flies like jet planes, it's very daring; and if you can't keep it, you will never have it. The *time is so sharp; sharper than a sharpen knife, that before blink it cuts the day into two, the month into three and the year into four; because, it's so fast.*

Time is so cunning, it deceives, it lures you into waiting for it; but for your turn it waits no more. More so, wasted times never come back neither are they regained. Moreover, according to Napoleon Bonaparte; ***"Space we can recover, but time never",*** and to a very high degree, you have to guide time or you become its merciless victim.

6

ORGANIZE YOUR EXPENSES

The chief motive for going into any venture (business) is to make profit that would trigger ones amount of wealth. More so, it's often perceived that only those who survive the pressure of business, by making their mark are only those said to be successful business owners.

Indeed, businesses or firms that operate based on principles of good (sound) management practice, such as separating company's account from Director's or Proprietor's individual's account or in other words, avoid letting your expenses overpass your (company's) profit, planning the strategies for winning, coordinating your activities, organizing your operations etc.

More so, if it's possible to take a good research on the failed companies so far, you would agree with me that, majority of them failed as a result of mismanagement that led to bankruptcy etc.

7

ITEMIZE YOUR OBSTACLES

Mr. Thomas Mayes Lewin (The founder and CEO) of T.M. Lewin™ started as a fashion designer in 1897 in Jermyn, London. Inasmuch as he was obsessed about quality and value hence; was prompted to found the TM Lewin clothing company in 1898. Since innovation was important to him, he worked harder to become one of the first companies to make the coat-shirt; the groundbreaking idea of a shirt with buttons down the front. Thomas Mayes realized *"that obstacles are not dead ends; neither are they determinants of failures, but modifiers of our inherent destiny in the present"*.

Indeed, today, T.M. Lewin™ is one of the world's largest manufacturers of tie and shirts; with an annual estimated production of 500,000 [Ties] and 2,000,000 [Shirts] units respectively (according to reports).

As a matter of fact, the owner of T.M. Lewin™ realized that you can take statistics of the world's problem and chose to be a solution.

8

EMBRACE CRITICISMS

"Small minds are the first to condemn great ideas"—John Mason. Besides, *it's only when you see the invisible that you can do the impossible; and that's only when your hope can become invincible.* Indeed, criticism may weigh one down, but constructive criticism is the bedrock of swimming out of the division of set goal. For instance, you might be wandering about in confusion due to lack of know-how etc, sort of, like what happened to Moses when he struck the rod, God had to criticize his action in order to save Aaron and the rest Israelites from the wraths of God.

Constructive criticism could quicken the pace of a confused leader or a follower. More so, destructive advice is as deadly as a weapon of warfare; while a constructively garnish criticism could put the path straight, smoothen the road and make the journey stress-free; because there is understanding between the critic and the criticized.

9

YOU'VE GOT TO BE DOGGED

Success is not a *take-and-wait* kind of, it's a *wait-and-take syndrome*; such that you have to take your time and strength to cultivate the investment, after which you "wait" for the investment to materialized before you can "get" hold of the promising benefits.

According to Napoleon Bonaparte; ***"To have ultimate victory, you must be ruthless".*** Besides, the road to the top is not smooth, but rugged; and any one who wants to take the lead must be dogged without fear of favour. For instance, when David learnt Goliath was terrorizing the Israelites, he (David) didn't take it with levity hence; dealt with Goliath without mercy or pity. ***"Those who seek to achieve things should show no mercy"*** . . . Napoleon Bonaparte.

10

CHOSE YOUR FRIENDS

There are two (2) kinds of friends:

1. The fair-weathered-friends and
2. The all-weathered-friends.

The former is/are the one(s) that help(s) you squander your money when you've gotten any, help kill your dream if you have one, always wishing you downfall, bringing you bad news always, never see good in anything you dream of, always tell you it's not possible etc while the latter are those kind of friends that encourage you, tell you it's possible, fault you wherever you are wrong and correct you, give you propulsion to scale through the obstacles of life, help you champion your dream till it sees the light of day. They never despise you; even when things are not easy, they stand by you through thick and thin etc. That was why it was said; *a true friend is better than a far brother or sister.*

11

PAINT YOUR WORLD

It's often said that, ***"It takes several kinds (class) of people to make a world"*** Douglas Jerrold. And the world is mostly dominated by those who are wise among the educated few.

Painting your world transcends the literal painting of anything by using colour(s) and brushes or rollers as the case may be. Painting your world means making an everlasting impact in the lives of people around you; taking advantage of the wisdom and knowledge you have in making sure you solve problems within your purview.

Your world is waiting for you to take hold of, and make judicious use of; for example, the Fashion Designers have their own world, so are the Musicians, the Pastors, the Movie Stars, the Lawyers, the Doctors etc; what matters is that, they all add values to their world via the problems they solve.

As a matter of fact, a lawyer's contribution to a sick person's health is as useless as a waste in a trashcan, but in his/her chamber, all legal problems are solved permanently etc. So, your world is waiting for you out there, go solve their problems; and I bet you God will richly bless you.

12

GUARD YOUR KNOWLEDGE

You could be the most creative artist who has a resounding gift of improvisation; but if you fail to bring in the artistic part of you, it were better you never acquired the skill(s). You need a great deal of polished knowledge to put your competitors' off-balance or off-guards; but it won't mean a thing, unless you know how to finish [the dream]. Do not be like some of the wiseacres or pretenders who presume they are wise with everything, unknowing they are fools in disguise.

Use your knowledge to paralyze your competitors, use your wisdom to cover up all mistakes you might make; and impress people with your aura of authority and creativity.

13

FIGHT YOUR FEARS

Fear is an enemy of success; fear could make a victor lose his victory; if he dares allow fright to mingle in between his concentration and focus. For example, Peters; when he was walking upon the waters to go meet Jesus at the other end of the river, he didn't sink from the start, but when he gave room to doubts that precipitated into fears hence; killed the zeal and focus he once had, and then started sinking into the water. Fear indeed, doesn't build; it breaks. Fear doesn't energize, it paralyzes.

Whenever fear grips you, it makes you feel destabilized, thereby waning your concentration and dissipates your accomplishing pace. Moreover, when you take time to fight your fears, by administering the right antidotes for a permanent solution—such as facing the fears one-after-the-other—by not giving in to doubts, being dogged and ruthless. According to Vergil *"They are able, because they think they are able"* and Thomas Fuller said something very salient, that; *"Brave actions never want a trumpet".* In this, when we can believe we are able to conquer our fears, I bet you, we wouldn't want our fears to cause mountains our faith can not remove.

Moreover, fears are like shadows, whenever we take a look at the mirror, we see images of ourselves in form of shadows; it usually goes with us to wherever; except we reshape our look to give the shadows our desired images; if not, the shape would remain unchanged whenever we visit the mirror. Besides, if we run from our fears, whenever we come in contact with them; they would increase and wait for us where we left them; to attack us whenever we let them.

14

STAND OUT

According to Claudius Appius Caecus; ***"Every man is the architect of his own fortune"*** and one man's misfortune bring to another man a fortune.

People are often troubled to make a choice of what they want their future to be like; sometimes, it's perceived by the weak and the lazy, ***that the best things in life are selected and reserved for a certain class of people***—which of course is a big L-I-E.

If you wish to be celebrated and reverenced, you must, stand to solve problems; and, ***the kind of problems determine the ovation you get; and the pay comes afterward***—the more demanding the problem solution, the more swelling your purse will be. It's not a matter of existing but adding values to the lives of people around you.

"People who are capable of thinking for themselves are those who will rarely be part of any herd"—Donald J. Trump; and ***it's pointless to have a great knowledge and keep it to yourself like a candle hidden under a covering***

Most people in the world today, are wishing manna could once again fall from heaven; and the others are blaming the governments for all their shortcomings etc. ***Everyone has money problems, some how to make the money, others how to keep it,*** **but** ***if you wish to stand out, solve problems***—by identifying one problem. Nokia® got into the telephoning industry; and changed the face of telecommunication, today; telephoning has grown to become tele-computing (telephone+computer) with such gadgets as the Bluetooth, infrared, USB [flash Drives] port, cameras and video player, JPEG, GPRS etc. The Nokia® Corporation has been able to solve people's problem of going to the cafés, going to the photo-studios etc; that's a good one for real, because they refused to be consumers; rather producers by solving people's problems.

15

BUILD A POSITIVE ATTITUDE

The right attitude can spring one up, but the bad one can fall any one faster than a push. Our attitudes are like the mirror with which people can access us, either good or bad. Our attitude is a function of our thoughts and our thoughts are products of our beliefs (imagination that breeds actions).

When our actions (attitude) become boring (repulsive) to people, it repels people from coming around us, but if it tells good of us, such as attracting people to us, it means a whole lot of transformation etc.

Attitudes are the custodians of our histories in the past, the image makers or secretaries of our present; and the clairvoyance (future-fortune-tellers) of our future; —that means, somebody's past can be known in the present and possibly reveals the future through such person's attitude.

Meanwhile, environmental influence could affect someone's attitude; such as wrong early foundation, people's opinion about such person etc.

Self image is another vital factor that determines the success or failure of any person. For example, if one has a negative influence etc, it's likely possible to affect the attitude (beliefs and actions etc). Paint a new picture of your present, in order to affect your future. Stop painting yourself in negative picture, see yourself succeeding, and speak positivism into your life.

More so, keep good companies; because the committee of friends has a lot to do in your life, either they kill your dream or build your world for the better. And above all; what you think matters.

16

ATTRACT SUCCESS

Life is not about consumption, but all about contribution; such as helping others to solve their problems etc.

Success and positive mindsets are akin to honey and honeycomb or likened to egg and its shell which of course are inseparable. Indeed, *success is a charm nobody resists no matter the circumstance surrounding the story;* it's obvious everybody wants to celebrate or identify with success.

Inasmuch as life and victory is concerned, we should never accept limitations or let people decide our boundaries—that's the only way we can secure success standpoint. Moreover, *"There's no royal road to learning, no short cut to the acquirement of any valuable art"* . . . Anthony Trollope. Besides, *"Hardship dictates the heights of the weak, but it's the instrument with which the wise get stronger"*.

There's no power or fame to be gained in letting go of the glory that it took you so long to build; and wait to live on the nick of time by the grace of favour. *To a great proportion, you must guard success or you will be the laughing stock of the dethroned failure.* There's for sure a better way to showcase and preserve your hidden treasure. *"It takes a great talent and skill to conceal one's talent and skill"* . . . La Rochefoucauld; and according to; Ovid, *"He lives well, who conceals himself well"*.

17

PRIORITIZE YOUR NEEDS

Needs are like clothes to be worn, you wouldn't out them all on, at once; because you have them all. For example, you can not put native material (Agbada etc) on to the bank or wearing the whole clothes you have at once,—it will look like madness in practice; and many people would read different meanings to it. You had better learn to prioritize your needs according to importance and not according pressure.

More so, we tend to forget what we should do and do others that are not necessary; thereby desiring most what we shouldn't. That means we fail to obey the laws of scale of preference in economics. Besides, you should also know that **"Genius is one percent inspiration and the rest is perspiration"** . . . Thomas A. Edison and becoming a genius, you must have the power to light your own fire.

Moreover, it's obvious that **wisdom is the gift of going to a party (being a guest) and knowing when to leave,** if you want to succeed in life; without wasting resources etc, you must prioritize your needs in order to cut unnecessary costs and still earn your intended result (goal).

18

PRAY ALWAYS

The holy Bible made us to understand that, *"It's not of him that runs nor of him that wills; but of God who shows mercy"*—Romans 9:16; I wish we all understand and know the efficacy of prayers to our everyday life. Whenever we want to pray, we shouldn't pray because we have problems, but we should do it like eating, it shouldn't be only when we are hungry . . . because God accepts our supplications with clean mind and whenever we thank God with praise; and present our petition before him with clean heart, for sure, He will meet all our needs. Also, *"The spirit also helps in our weaknesses; for we do not know what to pray about as we ought; but the spirit Himself makes intercession for us with groaning which can not be uttered"* . . . Romans 8:26.

Prayer is like seeking forgiveness and wishing its sustenance, it motivates us spiritually. More so, whenever we cry to God in prayers, He's there to rescue us from whatever danger . . . *"I will lift my eyes up to the hills where cometh my help"* and *"in my distress I cried to the lord and He heard me"* . . . Psalm 121:1, Psalm 120:1.

Prayer is a letter to God, in form of a request; asking God for a helping hand; and He will do everything for you according to request and faith. Prayer is the key to all situations and it's indeed, a key no door can withstand, because *he who ceases to pray ceases to prosper.*

19

CHALLENGE YOURSELF

Life is all about meeting needs either of others or for oneself, besides *"It must be considered that, there's nothing more difficult to carry out, nor more doubtful of success, nor more dangerous to handle, than to initiate a new order of things*—Niccolo Machiavelli.

As a matter of fact, life's about setting pace, living above board and make living more enjoyable; by taking upon yourself the responsibility to revamp the whole system of things as an initiator, pioneer and as a crusader of change for a better tomorrow. For example, nobody taught the moon and sun to shine, neither did any body taught God how to create; but due to His creative mindset, He made all things right at their own right time, because He was challenged with the way the earth was without form and void in the beginning.

"Do not let the negativity of life weigh you down". Do your best to move up to the next step of the ladder, I bet you; you can't be stopped by any force. Do not let people dictate your pace for you, neither wait and become a consumer, whereas your mates are busy contributing to the betterment of today and tomorrow.

Some few years ago, Barrack Hussein Obama was challenged to bring the kind of change America people deserved and looked forward to. More so, Adams Aliyu Oshiomole was challenged when he felt disappointed with the kind of politics the Edo state government was playing; hence he dared for a newness that brought him into the government house as the No. 1 citizen of the state (The Governor of Edo State, Nigeria).

20

FORECAST THE FUTURE

A good weatherman stays awake all night and work all day, studying the weather in order to predict the best weather. Many years ago in the Greek and Roman history, people were trained to study the weather by using the barometers to ascertain the temperature of the weather.

More so, studying the past in the present would enable us [to] predict the future by planning ahead of time. Being a good planner, would help us in our future pursuits. For example, if a farmer takes a close study of his/her past five years record of production against sales, he could easily project the sales forecast for the next year being the 6th year (Time Series).

Be the weatherman of your life; predict your future based on what your present has produced from your past.

21

QUIT PROCRASTINATION

Procrastination they say *is a **"Thief of precious time"**,* it's the process of dodging from responsibility or believing a miracle [for extra space of time] could come. Procrastination is very dangerous, it is the spirit behind many failed businesses today; it's often associated with the saying *"I will-do-it-later"* or *"there's-still-time mentality"* and at the end everything remains flopped by the flaws of some silly and uncontrolled waste of time.

Time is a veritable tool for business success; and when abused or misused, it could cripple the standing-business-once erected. As a matter of fact, there has never been any successful person who has never adhered to the principles of time.

Moreover, procrastination is an enemy of progress and should be without stress quitted; so that one can be focused in life and meet to the yearly, monthly or weekly tasks etc. procrastination is not a good way to learn anything in life; because it is not a good sauce for breakthrough. So abstain from procrastination for it buries one's dream before born.

You may have bright or brilliant ideas; but once you procrastinate, they may rarely see the light of day.

22

AIM HIGH, START SMALL

There is no harm in trying to start small in anything worth doing, either in life, business or otherwise. Indeed, I was meant to understand that nothing in life starts from the top (at the beginning) except the grave; and I believe no one wants to go there [go into the grave] now; because any candidate or partner of the grave is a dead person, ready to be buried; so don't be discouraged to start whatever career, by aiming higher—but start in a small measure, so you can grow faster.

More so, by aiming higher, you need to work extra harder in order to paint the picture of your future with which ever colour that pleases you. Indeed, aiming higher; one needs to have the expertise and strength in solving problems—because, the more problems you solve, will pave the ways for the more money you will command.

Many people today feel satisfied where they are, while some feel their present status is their starting point; a good example, is in the banking sector, some people wish to work in a banks forever, while some other wise ones dream and aim to own banks where the foolish among their peers could work to earn a living etc.

Aiming higher is not likened to become a longer-throat (glutton); that could become debility of mind which would also bring about financial or success decadence. Working harder by putting your mind, brain and hand to use could help the vision of reaching the zenith come to pass.

No hurry in life. Make judicious use of your time, talents and strength in becoming an enviable and indispensable asset than sitting somewhere and becoming a liability that will just end you up in consuming other people's sweat.

Starting small is not a sign of weakness or myopic mentality because; it enables you to see every bit of the dream and know where and when an expansion is needed, in order to build the summit with features that would stand the test of time; after all, ***Rome wasn't build in a day; and a million-miles' journey starts with a bold step.***

23

LEARN TO TAKE CONTROL

Taking control is much more than being a leader, because it's not every leader that has the courage and resilience (doggedness) to make his/her mark. Many "big-time" conglomerates etc; had been handcuffed by an irrevocable and unavoidable bankruptcy; simply for inability of the leaders to take their full place as the helmsmen and CEOs.

The eleventh day of September, two thousand and one (9/11/2001) has become indelible in the history of the world and especially the Americans who had relatives, friends etc that lost their lives during WTC (World Trade Centre) bomb blast and the pentagon Washington and New York (USA). During these periods of chaos and pains hence escalated the death toll by every passing hour amidst days. One thing for sure was certain that made the season unforgettable—that thing was *"learning to take control".*

President G.W. Bush, was indeed a true leader, a man that put all machinery in motion to make sure they stop the presumed frights, threats of recurrence of such awful experience—In this, President George W. Bush was visibly on ground, gave the Americans situation reports as they were without alterations etc, he was never taken away or weighed down by anxiety (was always calm), worked with the security operatives in making sure the lives of the people in America were safe and above all, as a leader he knew when to get back to the core-business of the day which was "administering governance" without fear or favour, but to the interest and betterment of the American people.

Another worth-remembering event that gave George Bush his mark as a leader with a difference was during the series of hurricanes and Tornadoes in America during his tenure as the helmsman of the American government. A true leader is a peace-lover, crusader of enabling environment etc, so that production can take place.

George Bush was a true icon of a leader; by doing his best in making sure peace reign in America, development triggered and bilateral relationships were cemented in order to extinguish any and every fire of war, hostility, chaos and conflicts etc within and outside the U.S.A. ***Taking control means taking total control"***

24

GUARD YOUR REPUTATION

Some people go to school to study history, some went to study news casting so they could read out history of inventors; while some other few hard workers are busy making histories. *Life is never a one sweet song, but necessity is the mother of invention;* join the bandwagon, be a crusader of history makers today.

Every success story makers could do anything to keep their story in tact, so that the memories could go a long way. Instead of being an onlookers, or readers of histories, who gets nothing than clapping for champions who had burnt their midnight oil and sweated by the day.

Reputation is a treasure, be careful not to lose it in a rush; carefully collect it, hold it (to be kept) for future use, most especially when you are establishing it or inventing it for the very first time. More so, make sure you hide your source because according to Albert Einstein; *"The secret to creativity is to know how to hide your sources"*

Moreover, your knowledge is your reputation. Keep it holy and sacred. *"Wear your learning, like your watch, in a private pocket; and do not pull it out; and strike it, merely to show that you have one . . ."* Lord Chesterfield. *Reputation is indeed a defense, when one loses it; his ladder of greatness is fallen faster than erected.*

25

BUILD YOUR SELF INTEREST

It's always in human nature to be attracted by that force which lifts us up; and repelled by those which bring us down or in the state of boredom; for example, a fisherman who really chose fishing from the desire of his heart, might not be moved to produce useful results if his job is changed to crop farming, simply for lost of satisfaction he derives from fishing. According to Ralph W. Emerson; *"That which we persist in doing becomes easier for us to do; not that the nature of the thing itself is changed, but that our power to do is increased."*

It's worth noting that, whenever you leave your self interest behind, you are actually leaving your destiny in limbo or dilemma; because **"Nothing great was ever achieved without enthusiasm"** . . . Ralph W. Emerson.

Self interest is the only lever that will move people when you make them see how you can in some ways, meets their needs or advance their course; but their resistance to your requests will magically fall away by killing the zeal in your enablement. Do not be intimidated. You have an uncommon and invaluable asset of knowledge to share—you will fill his coffers with rubies, and your wealth of understanding (talents etc) that is indispensable would make him live larger and happier than ever. In fact, according to Michihiro Matsumoto; *"Nothing is more costly than something given free of charge."*

26

CONTROL YOUR ANGER

Anger is akin to speed, without control, it kills sooner than saves. Anger is the most destructive of emotional responses, the more it increases, the more it clouds your vision and sense of concentration.

Never start a day or anything with anger, because it makes you feel less important or less privileged. *"A sovereign should never launch an army out of anger, a leader should never start a war out of wrath"* . . . Sun Tzu; *and "Wise men (should be) like coffers with double bottoms; which when others look into, being opened, they see not all that they hold"* . . . Sir Walter Raleigh.

Being dogged, ruthless etc mustn't necessarily mean [that] one must be angry; due to the fact that anger doesn't promote any facet of life instead it dissipates our pace of reaching perfection.

27

PLAN YOUR CHOICE

The choice you make today will either build or break your tomorrow; for example, if you do not want your clothes to smell, you have to wash them and if you wish them scent nice and last longer, you must wash them with soaps or detergent that has good smelling fragrance (scent) otherwise they might become rags overnight.

In life, we are the sculptors of our destinies. If we mould them well, many people would hardly resist us; they might not like our faces, names or religions but can't help running after us (coming close to us); simply for the sake of our beautiful future—having been moulded with the best of resources and painted with the most attractive colours (expertise) and become more aesthetically irresistible.

Do not make a choice in a rush, no matter the pressure or anxiety, try to be in a relax mood before taking any action or decision; no matter the magnitude of importance or viability; because reputation is a treasure; and making the wrong choice could kill it faster than notice.

As a matter of fact, it's very wrong and ungodly to do anything unconsciously; indeed, ***"It's no use living and not know why you are existing".*** That's mostly why God gave us freedom of choice; such that when God forces us to accept His choice without our freewill to chose; thereby, when anyone loses or fails, he may end up blaming God for forcing him/her against his/her wish of choice; but now you are on your own, as I am on mine whenever we are to make our choices.

28

COMPLACENCY

Complacency kills growth. Complacency and procrastination are like husband and wife—the former is the spirit of satisfaction (being ok with where you are or what you have) whereas, there are still much works to be done, that could Better shape one's tomorrow; but, due to fears of advancing forward and daring obstacles, the person may decide to be stagnated. While the latter's failure or downfall is built around its inability to defeat the spirit of delay. [i.e *I-will-do-it later* etc.] So whoever that chooses to win must do everything possible to fight temptations arising from complacency and or its cohorts, by becoming aggressively ruthless.

Many people's businesses today are battling with survival; for feeling and believing they have arrived or made it real big; then became satisfied where they were— never to move up or get better. Indeed, laziness is one factor associated with complacency. Besides, the major threats accompanied by the dilemma of complacency are:

- Fear of the unknown
- Inexperience
- Investment myopia
- Growth unconsciousness
- Laziness etc.

Indeed, complacency really kills when we allow these five (5) factors of complacency rob our lives, business and other careers of our benefits etc.

29

BE CHANGE-CONSCIOUS

Honesty plays a very salient role in changing from one course of action to another. Honesty is the best and safest way to disarm the spirit of negativism and distraction in order to unleash the powers of our hidden treasure.

Since success or victory is never received or given freely, someone else must have paid the price that you enjoy. Inasmuch as, variety is the spice of life hence, change makes the difference.

Shining more brightly beyond those around you could be more than just a wish, but a skill inherently nurtured to sing you praise at your gate. Skills like you have got, is so uncommon to so many mediocre and weaklings; since you were born with or acquired this uncommon traits (skill) etc, you had better enhance them, learn to attract positive attention from success recorded and above all, learn to keep your success story, so it could linger forever. Honesty for sure is a defense, but when one loses it, one becomes exposed to his/her foes; thereby his/her source becomes reveal to numerous competitors etc.

> *Change is a law of life, those who look at the past and the present are certain to miss the future*—J.F. Kennedy

30

LEARN FROM
PEOPLE'S MISTAKES

The best and safest way to right our wrongs is by correcting our mistakes; but the worst and most dreaded action is for one to be conscious not of his mistakes or errors of others.

According to one of the world's most funeral orator, Thucydides . . . *"I fear our mistakes far more than the strategies of our enemies"*; and *"The wise courses are to profit from the mistakes of others"*. Terrence. And to John Dryden, in a book titled, *'All for love'*, said; *"Errors, like straws upon the surface flow"*. Aaron knew that if mistakes are noticed yet not amended, it could show a Christian heaven's gate; but prevent entrance. That was simply why he learnt from the grievous and precarious mistake made by his predecessor. (Moses) when he was unable to control his [hot] temper.

Everyman must decide whether he will walk in the light for correcting the errors of his predecessors, or living in total darkness for allowing his mistakes (by failing to right the wrongs he had seen to grow into fearful terror etc).

More so, let's stop blaming others for their erroneous actions; because it kills our spirit of advancing forward (courage). According to Robert Anthony; *"The best way to escape from our problems is to solve them"*.

Mistakes are like fire, if you let them have their way, you might not be able to put them off or control them." More so, **"Better be wise by the misfortunes of others than by your own"** Aesop.

31

DON'T LOOK
DOWN ON YOURSELF

In 1920s, Ethiopia recorded a historic or one of the most memorable eras during the reign of warlord, Haile Selassie (Ras. Tafari). Selassie, who felt there was none like him (bold and fearless), until Balcha Dejazmach dared him (selassie). The rest contenders like cowards bowed and surrendered to Haile Selassie—but there was one man who saw it as unreasonable to give in to threats, resulting from attempted murder by sellassie in 1927 to be specific.

Despite outnumbered times invitation amidst cooked-up tricks to strip him (Balcha) off his title, in order to dethroned him. In all, Selassie failed to carry out his stratagems and gimmicks on him.

Indeed, selassie and Balcha were much at loggerheads during the late 1920s than any other times in history; but because Balcha was very wise; he refused to be silenced or pushed aside like the other contenders that Selassie used as scapegoats.

According to Napoleon Bonaparte; *"To have ultimate victory, one must be ruthless"*; and Sir Walter Raleigh said, *"Wise-men (should be) like coffers with double bottoms, which when others look into, being opened, they see not all that they hold"*. Don't sell your hopes; take courage as you look up! Hop up! Dust yourself and move to the next level like Balcha did.

Courage, according to Billy Graham . . . is *"when a brave man takes a stand, then, the spine of others are often stiffened"*. Don't be scared to stand your ground; it might not be easy, but for sure victory shall surface when you refuse to quit or give up. Besides, God is more interested in your end than the beginning; indeed, *braveness tears down the walls of fear and builds up the house of greatness.*

32

BE THE BEST IN ALL

Being the best or becoming the most-sought-after by all who knows your value or expertise is not a mere sit-and-wish approach; but, requires a great deal of putting the hand and brain to work. Since, *we know that things can't change to the way we want them, why not let's change our ways to suit what the time demands.*

Moreover, *since we can't do great things, why not let's do small things in great ways;* moreover "*Defeat should never be a source of discouragement, but rather a fresh stimulus*"—South.

Meanwhile, discretion is essential in bringing out the best in us; and the power of our youthfulness, the loudness of our voices, the beauty of our creativities are all what would send us afar above our equals; *"The heights by great men reached and kept, were not attained by sudden flight, but they, while their companions slept, were toiling upward in the night."* . . . Longfellow.

More so, *"All human activities either success or failure is prompted by desire"*—Bertrand Russell, this has been the source behind Tiger Wood's success story; as one of the world's most respected golfer ever.

Being the best in all; is always the most adored choices every man has to make, but majority ends up wishing. Don't forget that, *"He lives well, who conceals himself well"*—Ovid.

33

GIVE MORE TO GET MORE

According to George Allen, *"If you want to catch more fish, use more hooks"*, and the bible says, *"To whom much is given, much is expected"*.

Giving, in all is very broad and it covers all spheres of human life—but in this case, I mean giving your resources (time, money, attention etc) for the growth of whatever your pursuit is; for example, it's sure for every worker who works overtime to get paid much more than the usual or regular pay etc.

As a matter of fact, whenever you give, it's like victory, it pops you up like a conqueror; but when you are at the receiving end, it makes you feel dejected or the conquered. Giving much helps to reshape your world for a better bumper harvest; the bible in the book of 2Corinthians 9:6 says, *"Whoever gives bountifully must surely receives a bumper proceeds; and whoever sows sparingly wouldn't get anything but miniature (meagre) harvest;* Simply for the fact that, whatever you give is what measures your receipts—and whatever you see is what you have gotten.

Moreover, to conquer or dominate in wars, more soldiers (troupes) have to be deployed to overwhelm the invaded cities or territories, couple with sophisticated ammunitions.

34

BE INSPIRED BY
OTHER PEOPLE'S SUCCESS

Mahatma Gandhi is one of the world's most respected, diplomatic conflicts resolution expert (without arms or ammunition but dialoguing process) who gave Martin Luther King Jr. a boost to resolving conflicts without rancour, besmirch, frowns etc. Martin Luther was indeed a good learner of good things, thereby threading the success story of Mahatma Gandhi in making sure his dream of winning more party members in the labour force (the non-violent protests etc).

Not until 1965 when Martin Luther had his first and one of the world's most successful gathering in Washington DC, where he had about 250,000 people in attendance; The *'I have a dream speech'.* Martin Luther's mediatorship and oratory prowess were seemingly guided by Mahatma Gandhi's dialoguing charisma and eloquence skills etc.

More so, many people's breakthrough today had been the close and fervent study of great people's successes. For example; great people like Bill Williams Gates, Warren Buffet, Donald J. Trump etc, had always wanted to break the fence of setbacks in the financial circle, Bill Cosby, Whoopi Goldberg, Will Smith etc had also worked assiduously to soar above the limitations of the ordinary world; by blazing the trail in the make-believe-act in art.

Moreover, because Martin Luther King Jr. ***knew that wars are poor chisels to carving out our peaceful tomorrow,*** **and** ***we are not makers of history but we are made by history;*** *He was* propelled to make an impact. Besides, if we can't learn from other people's mistakes or being inspired by the successes of greater men and women; it means the hope of our better tomorrow is burning away like the stick of a cigarette.

35

NO UNDERESTIMATION

The force that led to the fall of Goliath wasn't the spirit of victory in David alone, but the pride and over-exaggeration that led to David being underestimated by the so-called giant Goliath. Besides, no body is an island or a monopolist of strength or victory.

As a matter of fact, *victory is not measured in a rush; until after the fights (contests), thereafter emerge the winners;* because, in football or any game, no team should be underrated or else the big teams that are underestimating other smaller ones might get the shocker of their lives.—It's often said; *it's not over until it's over (that's when the final whistle is blown).*

The bible made us to understand something that; *pride goes before a fall,* that was exactly what broke the strength of Goliath the Philistine. Because *reputation is a goldmine, it shouldn't be allowed to be contaminated by enemies; or else we soon lose it than winning.*

Indeed, do avoid looking down on any person, group of persons, countries, companies etc because, if we are to go by size as a means to measuring strength, America wouldn't be the world most powerful country today, but *because it's not by might, not by power nor about how we feel, but how it should be.*

36

BE BOLD

"Few are born bold; some become bold by experience and many live, eat and die with cowardice"

When David heard of one stubborn, uncultured, huge, threatening Philistine named Goliath, he wasn't timid to take the centre stage when the battle line was drawn. At a time he (David) knew the fight wasn't for weaklings neither was it for mediocre nor feeble minded hence, he became brave as a true warrior that he was; inferiority complex left him, forthwith strength gripped him and the balm of victory quicken his fainting courage, then he began to see Goliath as an ordinary uncircumcised Lilliputian from the tribe of Philistine.

You must practice and develop your boldness, build your courage, enhance your skills and increase your source of strength. Most of us are timid hence, we want to avoid tension by all means; and dodge from obstacles that might lead to confusion or fears of failures. Above all, we wished to be chosen and reverenced by all—All these require our boldness to open the doors of enviable greatness. Because a *"Nation on civilization that continues to produce soft-minded men, purchases its own spiritual death on the installment plan"*—Martin Luther. *So "If we want to achieve victory we should be ruthless"*—Napoleon Bonaparte.

37

RESIST DISTRACTIONS

We are often terrified by the fear of making mistakes, what people would say of us and other mind-threatening, thought provoking questions such as; The enmity we might enkindle; if we extend our limit of usual status, What if we make flaws? How do we remedy these erroneous actions etc could becomes our fears and mind obsessions etc.

Moreover, we must not feel trepidation or depression within us whenever we seem to be facing or seeing temptations that could bring in confusion as a result of distraction etc. Indeed, no matter the premonition, diverted attention or something of some sorts that could cause lost of attention or direction. For example, when the Republican Presidential Aspirant (USA) in 2003 John Kerry lost his dream of president to the incumbent President George W. Bush, he wasn't seeing his defeat as a dead-end; neither did he see the poll as an aspersion, but an opportunity to taste the U.S. election in the presidential level.

According to Henry Ford, *"Failure is the only opportunity to begin more intelligently;* and Mike Murdock said; *"Success will smile at the man who refuses to be down at the corridor of failure".*

Besides, *"It's only when we can see the invisible that we can do the impossible"*—Anonymous; and above all, don't let your weakness cost you your destiny; so stand firm and resist all forms of distraction.

38

MOVE WITH THE LIGHT

The wave makers of today world-wide, may not have been the most aged, most religious, most educated etc; but people whose yesterday's hardships couldn't send packing, people whose yesterday's tremour couldn't freeze, people whose past fire couldn't consume, men whose past ignorance couldn't infest, women whose yesterday's errors couldn't deter from pressing forward etc.

According to Charles Darwin (Geneticist) ***"It's not the strongest of the species that survives nor the most intelligent, but the most responsive to change"*** (*The light*). Most of the champions of today are those who ruthlessly defend what they knew (talent etc), at the end they stood out in the crowd.

The richest men and women of today are the most intelligent. (Not brilliant), the ones who were able to solve yesterday's problem with today's expertise; in order to better tomorrow. More so, majority of today's exemplary leaders and role-models are those people who wouldn't allow their mistakes weigh them down; rather they fought all predicaments and distracters without fear of ignorance; but with hopes of victory. These were men and women whose strengths and directions were driven by their passion for a resounding success.

39

HAVE A STYLE

No man will ever survive the hitches of today's hardship-infested world unless he changes from what he does to something else; and stop being satisfied with where he is, but to start seeing or thinking of where he long for. Besides, *"No man is ever whipped until he quits in his mind"*—Napoleon Hill and *"A man can't ride your back unless it's bent"*—Martin Luther, these mean that you are not permitted to fail or retrogress, unless you throw in the towel or give in to doubts.

Having a style is more than sowing or buying styled (sewn) clothes; rather, it's the spirit of standing out among one's equals. For example, St. Michaels® clothing company noticed everybody has things in common in the fashion (clothing) industry; hence has to define their couture for the satisfaction of men by introducing the *"Marks & Spencer™"* clothes and inner wears (briefs, sleeveless, etc) and ties (neck ties) and a host of other body enhancing products. Marks & Spencer™, an arm of St. Michaels® has been existing since the mid 19th century, yet still a name that has made a mark in the fashion or clothing industry; simply for having a defined standard that is matchless.

Moreover, moving fast is not the same thing as going somewhere, and no matter how slow you might be going, please ensure you get to your destination no matter how long it takes you. In fact, according to George Allen; *"The achiever is the only individual that's truly alive"* and those who couldn't succeed or survive the tremour of competitions etc were presumed to have been buried in the business world. Besides, *"A real idea keeps changing and appears in many places"*—Mason Cooley, all these to satisfy mankind etc.

40

MASTER YOUR DESIRES

Mastering a desire or talent could be much more than just perform-and-win basis; rather, it could exceed the usual play-and-win mentality—such was what drove the passion behind David's interest when he chose to be a singer (Music Composer, instrumentalist) etc.

Singing a song could mean exerting of energy and mental prowess. Emphatically, it demands a calculative attention and creative mental synergy. David was indeed a devoted songwriter, dedicated song singer—all to give glory to God Almighty. David was indeed moved by the burning passion he has for song—not just any song, but songs that gave praises to the name of Jehovah Almighty.

Moreover, Great Edson Arantes Do Nascimento (a.k.a. King Pele of Brazil) is another replica of a passionate servant of thirsty desires to do what he likes best; and that thing was *"Football"*. Unlike David, he couldn't sing neither could he act moves like Arnold Schwarzenegger or Will Smith, nor could he dance like the late king of pop, Michael Jackson (of blessed memory), but he stood his ground, got his mind made up to defend football till the end of his time; and today he (Pele) is celebrated as an icon in the world of football.

Mastering one's desire or harnessing one's resources into becoming a productive channel wouldn't only bring joy to the producer or generator; but also to the receptors or the people at the receiving end whose needs have been met. Indeed, ***many people are just to God like a baker's dozen; whereby they just exist without knowing why they do so,*** which is against God's wish for us; besides, it's no use living and do not have a positive impact on the lives of people around your dwelling place.

41

BE A PRODUCER, NOT A CONSUMER

Often times, weak people are threatened by the wind of hardship; they sit at home everyday, end up wishing the government could provide them with all basic needs of life, including their personal problems solutions etc. Sometimes, *the most lazy people are those that want or wish for the best things in life*—such as comfort, luxuriant living without sweat or stress.

Since cutting edge technology has made life simpler, better and more affordable hence, the hardworking few are sticking their necks to breakout from the dungeon, hardship and grip of poverty; but most of other people are swimming in the pool of complacency and cash-strap assumed assets, due to ignorance. For instance, in the late nineteenth to mid-twentieth century; the wide use of the world wide Web (WWW) Internet Access, General Packet Radio Service (GPRS), Wireless Satellite, VSAT etc were not much rampant; if not totally absent (in some parts of the world); but with the relentless efforts of people who wished to see the best of lives lived before death—These people nurtured their ideas and they became realities.

Why sit at home and condemn the government or other people's effort or inventions; when you can hardly make a dish out of a meal. Join the bandwagon today, *be productive not according to your wish but according to your ability;* after all, these few trailblazers are not ghosts;

neither do they have two heads, so be useful not only to yourself but to others.

Moreover, if you make up your mind, you could become the next to move the world from where it's now to where we want it to be. Join the league of exceptional people; people who are busy trying to change the world for the better in the best of their abilities. For instance; someone puts his expertise and courage to see the beauty of life; by creating software (programs) that would better lives—for example, people created (invented) the Digital Video Disc player (DVD player), Personal Computer (PC) cell phones etc, all these are to bring comfort and more enriched lives for the humankind.—You; on your own, what have you done so far? Stop being a consumer today, become a producer. Add value to people's lives; you will be glad you did.

42

SOLVE PROBLEMS

Our successes in life are not determined by our certificates, degrees, awards etc neither are our greatness in life precipitated by our age, culture, religion, sex or our course of study; but by bringing our I.Q (Intelligent Quotient) to bear; such as making use of our knowledge and ability—together to effect the difference. For instance, most people go to school to study how to pass (their) exams, tests and get good grades, but I must tell you this, the richest people today may not have been the people with the best grades as at yesterday. Moreover, not that good grade is bad, but good grade from a dull (brilliant but-not-intelligent) brain without creative spirit can't do anything with the certificates or good grades.

The difference between intelligence and brilliance is that, the former can improvise in difficult situations; while the latter can do nothing than give you what you gave to it (i.e. copycat, photo-reproduction) which wouldn't change anything. A good example is, for instance in a class where these two sets of candidates are in, and an exam question is set such as; (Q).what ways are means of traveling abroad (USA from Nigeria to be specific)? Options; (A) by car, (B) by donkey (C) by ship. Naturally, the correct option is C which is ship since there's no airplane, but the most brilliant amongst the two will decide not to mark or chose any option because he/she was taught that the only means of traveling abroad is by air, via airplane by his/her tutor; unknowing that there are two ways to answering questions—the right way and the wrong way. But because the second student was intelligent, he/she would quickly chose the correct option amongst the selected options.

Meanwhile, it's only those people who can think for themselves (the intelligent); the ones who can solve problems, people who can use Intelligent Quotients to solve quantitative problems such as manipulations (improvisation) etc, are the only ones who can stand taller beyond their equals in the times of needs.

More so, remember always that, ***the people that want to succeed must solve other people's problem or else they will be overwhelmed by the hardship of today.*** And always know that the kind of solutions you rendered determine your pay, so if you want to have a big or huge take-home-cash, you had better learn to solve more mind-cracking & brain-searching problems or questions.

43

BE DYNAMIC

Dynamism is one core part of creativity that can breed breakthrough. For example, some people learn so fast, that they even end up teaching others; and some learn from other people's flaws' in order to prevent themselves from repeating the same mistakes. Besides, it's often said in Africa that; *"A wise man wouldn't enter the stream with two legs in at once; but fools do"*.

As a matter of fact, one person must bear the brunt of another; by paying the debt of another (person), that's why, no matter how you may try to steal from nature without balancing the equation; (such as by taking short cuts etc.) thereby leaving one's life to remain stocked in limbo. However, *"A church's debt is always the devil's salary"*- Henry W. Beecher.

Indeed, the end is what decides who wears the crown; because according to Henry W. Beecher, *"We are all rich or poor but according to what we are; not according what we have"*. Besides, education doesn't give job, neither does certificates bring money (without knowledge), rather education breeds certificate (and certificate in-turn is a product of our education that's a means to our end), the end they say justifies the means.

In fact, your dynamism gives you an edge over your equals in your line of avocation; because, your education or knowledge had taught you how and when (time) to strike when it's business hour (that's the I.Q. I have always talked about). Life is what we make of it; it's not who starts first or lasts but who carries the day.

44

BEAR THE SHAME

How much do you know of great people? Do you know their pasts; if you are reading their presents? You have to take the courage to face the turmoil; no matter the level of shame—since it can't be avoided, it must be with patience endured.

Do you know that every record breaker once had to bear some shames before his/her scar became a star? It's true that every great man or woman that is up there today must have had an ugly and horrible past. Besides, once we know the question, solve the equation—I bet you, the answer wouldn't be farfetched due to the knowledge of the crown after the tussle.

Not withstanding the hardship experienced during the toiling time. It's certain that no hard worker [that] wouldn't be rewarded according to his sweat. Indeed, I would call the hard times *"the planting season"* and after which comes the harvest.

Shames are like the road way to the top, (success), they are crowns in disguise; no matter how they may come or appear, but once one can overcome the trepidations, bear the shame, resist quitting etc; I bet you, God wouldn't want to forsake you. A good example was Christ's life on earth; he suffered afflictions, betrayal, tortures and a host of unbearable psychological, spiritual and physical humiliations. When he (Christ) was passing through test (water and fire) he didn't feel regrets in him; neither did he blame God for all the sufferings, rather he kept on committing himself to the selfless service; because he knew his reward was greater than anything material or whatever money can buy. (The crown of eternal glory).

Shames are the bridges you must cross to get to your destination (stardom), but when you allow the shame to linger for too long, it then becomes your fault.

45

NO STOPPING, KEEP MOVING

Often times, we feel unsafe to swim in the stream of today's business world and scale through; yeah! It's true; due to the nature of frightening omen and signs of fears that bring weaknesses; but never to worry because; a focused mind wouldn't stop by the way until its destination is reached.

No matter how people may laugh at you, or mock you because you have fallen or fell, but what matters is what you wish or think about your success. A typical example was that of our lord (Jesus Christ) when he was teaching his disciples; some amongst the Jews asked him, *"Who are you?"* and he (Jesus), replied *"Who do you think I am?"* (I am the lord, the Son of God, the king of kings . . .).

So, since Christ knew whom he was, where he was going to, he wasn't scared of the earthly turmoil; neither was he afraid of their wickedness.

Stopping by the way is not bad but failing to continue the journey till finish is cowardice; so keep on the struggles for the simple reason that crowns are not for the feebleminded, mediocre etc; but the best is for those who refuse to quit, even when the journey gets tougher. According to Mike Murdock *"Success will shine at that man who refuses to be down at the corridor of failure"* and, be up and doing; never let the negativity of the world or hardship of today bring you down or dictate your height in life (for you).

46

EMBRACE EXCELLENCE

There's no limit to the height or success of any man whose mind is made up on greatness, but the person's goals are determined by the creativity and positive-mindedness of the conceiver or pursuant of such idea.

There's no telling you how much you can go or reach; if only you'd put in your very best to see that your pursuit is not merely to succeed or win, but to keep the winning or success spirit intact. More so, some people got to fail after getting close to the ladder whose steps bear success, due to their failure to hold onto the spirit of excellence in the form of perfection. For example, God created the earth, and noticed there wasn't light and there was no dry land (imperfect) hence, he renewed his mind and caused everything to change for good; and at last it became perfect (land separated from waters (rivers), day separated from night etc); Genesis 1:

Indeed, there are some persons who enjoy doing things half way, haphazardly etc, without trying to pursue excellence via success etc. No matter what you do, your career, occupation etc; it's very expedient you know that there's reward in doing things excellently; after all, God (our maker) is excellent.

In fact, we must not be told to do good things before we do them, we must not be rebuked for doing bad or unacceptable things before we stop or desist from them.

Let's be up and doing, loving what is but excellent because we are God-like.

Do not be moved by evil-mindedness, attracted by ungodly gains, destructive applauds etc. For example, many people engage themselves in the production of substandard drugs, body care products, importation of expired and adulterated health care and skin care products etc. If you are not enemies of national growth, saboteurs of government's campaigns etc why won't you be patriotic enough to stand out, by shunning anything that wouldn't bring glory to God and your family. Desist from unwholesome practices that could cause pains to the people next to you etc.

Embrace excellence today, so substandard products could be far from us and completely eradicated.

47

BE CONFIDENT

"Of all the disorders of the soul; envy is the only one no one confess to"—Plutarch.

Boldness they say strikes fear; and the fears break the strength of confidence in any man. Whenever you get discouraged your powers shrink, but whenever you exhume guts, the deadened cells and nerves in you would resurrect and function with fresh stimulus.

When you are confident of your ability and knowledge, the picture is quite clear from the negative to the finished-positive; by polishing and preserving the beauty of your outcomes, simply for knowing whom you are, what you do and the peak of your destination.

More so, avoid doing things haphazardly and whenever you do anything, make sure you do it as an expert and a special person that you are—such that whenever troubles or difficulties creep in, you wouldn't become confused or running from pillar to post because of lack of the know-how; but when you are able to fight the challenges with your expertise (confidence and know-how); you will find a genuine breakthrough that no scale can measure.

Timidity infects people with awkward energy; elicits embarrassment and exacerbate mistakes due to the tension of the frights; hence creates a vacuum in the accomplishment of our ambitions. More so, lack of confidence precipitates inferiority complex and thereby creates room for doubts and worries (anxiety); this without delay kills a dream before it's dreamt.

It's often perceived that experience is a wall of defense to confidence; and according to Cardinal Richelieu *"Experience shows that, if one foresees from far away the designs to be undertaken; one can act with speed when the moment comes to execute them".*

48

COLOUR YOUR CHOICES

Men are so simple of mind, and so much dominated by their immediate needs, that a deceitful man will always find plenty, who are ready to be deceived, . . . Niccolo Machiavelli.

Artists and artistes are the best set of liars; the former give you wrong gifts but paint or wrap them with colourful and irresistible coverings (package); while the latter are ready to dramatize scenes of make-the-audience believe they are all real; unknowing they were staged.(deceit of the highest order)

Indeed, do not have the fear of making mistakes; because, whenever you do, the boat of your victory of painting the choice would fasten its anchor on the way to sinking. Fear of mistakes shouldn't be entertained in your imagination, due to your calculations and the popular saying in art (creative) that *"Every mistake is a design"*.

Moreover, whenever you want to do the colouring, please; make sure you do it [by] yourself; in order to suit your desires and serve the chief aim of its inception; in other words, if you give it to someone else to do, the person might do it against your wish—its aesthetic value would be debased and your reputation soured. Mind you, colours are innumerable, but it's whatever colour you desire that would speak out the beauty.

Besides, according to David Hume *"No man needs despair of gaining converts to the most extravagant hypothesis who has art enough to represent it in favourable colours".* Moreover, *"If you want to tell lies that will be believed; don't tell the truth that won't"*— *Emperor Tokugawa Ieyasu.*

Colouring your choices is one of the most creative concept any great thinker can think of, for example; it's no more new or strange to see the manner every company tries to brand or re-brand their products with new packaging techniques; such that the consumers or end-users may see it/them as new formula or new products; unknowing they (companies) have been playing on their (consumers') intelligence—For changing their products and advertisement pattern or channels; the hunger-for-the-products gets the consumers carried away; yet gets them running after the old-but-re-branded-assumed-new products; *that's indeed a big lie that was painted with truth and real colours of packaging;* and that was exactly why Adolf Hitler said *"Make the lie big, make it simple, keep saying it, and eventually they will believe it"* in this, colour is your medium of selling your choice to the outside world.

49

BE COMMITTED

Being committed in the pursuit of success or greatness is akin to a marriage; whereby the two parties (bride and groom) have to put in their very best in terms of love (affection) unity, appreciation of each other, acknowledging that none is indispensable; hence they become synergized in practice. It's obvious that, one flower however, cannot make a beautiful garden; and being committed to achieve any set goal or dream would propel one to become more energetic, focused, distinctive and head-on.

By giving all the resources, (attention, materials skills) etc would give one a step ahead; not minding the chaos or troubled waters that might surface in the future. Commitment is like giving the best gift at the right time; hence you put the recipient under obligation, such as becoming tamed or under your tutelage without fear of misdirection etc.

When you give all you have and do it with the whole of your heart, the reward is usually beyond expectation. Knowledge; according to Joseph Addison ***"Is indeed, that which is next to virtue, truly and essentially raises one man above another";*** So if you wish to be raised above your equals, you had better be more committed to whatever that you are doing today. Wear your passion or gift like belt to your waist, so your trousers wouldn't fall off.

As a matter of fact, it takes but a perfect person at a perfect time to make a perfect impact in his/her generation;

the perfect time is now and that perfect person is you. Despite the wealth of experience you may have acquired, there are no two ways or short cuts to troubled waters, due to the fact that life is no bed of roses; move on, bear the upheavals, keep on the goal-aiming mission; you will get hold of it . . . If only you refuse to quit.

50

AVOID MONEY TEMPTATION

Indeed, money is a defense or power house to those who have it; and it brings those men who lack it intimidations by those who have gotten it. In fact, money is like weapon of warfare to the people who have acquired it; but in this; great care has to be taken in order to avoid the temptation of being ruined by quest for money powers; as does the influence of speed that kills.

Money indeed is a good servant, but not a good master; because if one doth make money or financial gains his/her utmost proceeds, such a person may soon be evicted from the standpoint of financial success; due to the uncontrolled quest for wealth (avarice).

Money has broken so many relationships, it has soured so many prospects due to its domineering spirit and betrayal syndrome; for example, the uncontrolled appetite for money was what made Judas Iscariot betrayed Jesus Christ of Nazareth. Indeed, that was why the bible book of 1Timothy 6:10 condemned *the love of money, as the root of all iniquities.* Let your deeds be trustworthy, let your actions be unquestionable either monetarily or otherwise because; *"Money is never spent to so much advantage as when you have been cheated out of it"*—Arthur Schopenhauer.

Money is irresistible; its temptation could make any man lose his/her direction if he loses focus. *Learn to be that man, whom the spirit of money wouldn't intoxicate, that woman whom the temptation of pride wouldn't overwhelm. Be that fellow, whom the power of greed wouldn't consume, learn to be that person, who wouldn't do anything mischievous; all for the sake of amassing wealth at the detriment of another fellow (human).* Learn to build a good name with an invaluable reputation; that would attract noblemen near and far to you. Good name according to Shakespeare *"Is the immediate jewel of the soul of any man or woman".*

51

DEPEND ON PATIENCE

Success is not a journey for the weak, neither is victory a game for mediocre or the timid; but for those (people) who are embodiments of breakthrough via versatility and creativity. To achieve any goal or set any enviable standards, you must pay the price of bravery and doggedness; so you could fall the walls of every militating obstacles. There should be no-mercy-syndrome; such that, the pace is kept high out there without fear of deviation or distraction.

Indeed, Kautilya; an Indian philosopher once said something very salient about achieving greatness; that, ***"Those who seek to achieve things should show no mercy"***. Moreover, do not be modeled by the pattern of life around you that are inconsequential to your growth, rather erect a wall of defense to build your career distinctively. As a matter of fact, refuse to be weak or blinded (creative-wise). Renew yourself by shaping a new identity for your future; refuse to be tossed around by difficulties resulting from inferiority complex or mediocrity, learn to stand firm on what you know is right or whatever you believe in.

Avoid being weak, because weak people; according to Cardinal De Retz; ***"(Weak people) never give way when they ought to"***. Simply for fear of taking the bull by the horns or acting against all odds irrespective of what or who is involved. More so, never seem to be in a hurry—***"Hurry*** *indeed, is a product of fear and fear is an end-product of cowardice that justifies failure".*

Learn to be patient, no matter the magnitude of the expectations or the velocity of the process; one thing for sure is that *"All is well that ends well"* and *all wound must be healed, only by time (patiently).* The secret of great powers lie in unflinching persistence and unwavering patience; no matter what.

52

DUPLICATE YOUR STRENGTH

"It must be considered that there's nothing more difficult to carry out, nor more doubtful of success, nor more dangerous to handle, than to initiate a new order of things"—Niccolo Machiavelli.

Duplicating of strength is the utmost creative mentality in a bid to surviving the today's business needs or entrepreneurial demands. For instance, as an entrepreneur, one needs to apply the spirit of team work—whereby everybody is involved. Enhance the pace of success by introducing *Train-the-Trainers program*—in which, you will have to train more hands in order to help you meet the pressing demands.

Wisdom is a product of reasoning, it's not taught in high schools; neither is it transferred from one who has it to another who is deficient of it. According to Lord Chesterfield; *"Knowledge is a comfortable and necessary retreat and shelter for us in advanced age; and if we do not plant it while young, it will give us no shade when we grow old".* As a matter of fact, *no man survives in solitude or progresses by standard of self-judgments.*

Unity is strength, and any one, who wishes to make a mark; or live above boards, should learn to be adaptive in copying what the trend holds. More so, it's a known fact that, the beauty and strength of the broomsticks is in their unity. When you train your subordinates, team-mates etc, the burdens become reduced to the best possible level, due to the wisdom of being a creative leader. Duplicating of strength, talents or ideas is like planting a seed, and when it's its harvest time the glory will go to the sower.

According to Dr. Samuel Johnson, ***"Solitude is dangerous to reason, without being favourable to virtue"***. Avoid being selfish—only fools are selfish or stingy with their gifts; do not forget that when you have; give to those that would be of importance to you in the future—because if you fail to give or teach those under your supervision, it should be known by you that, you are not killing their dreams or delaying their destinies, but also destroying your future; because, ***"Whatever that affects the yolk of an egg must also affect the albumen"***.

53

SHARPEN YOUR EGO

How much do you know of your personality, do you know your amazing power could influence the nobility, project an unquestionable success and irresistible sense of confidence; that could attract attention from far and near [and from all and sundry]?—In this, you must play the tactics of *self-assurance* as that of young Abraham Lincoln; before he made himself a world-famous political icon that had triggered people's faith for success worldwide.

Indeed, learn to carry yourself above all around you; by virtue of your charismatic mediatorship—but, do not become obsessed or driven by the spirit of pride or arrogance; lest, they will both repel people against you, due to the attitude you possess. Besides, do always remember to employ your *defensive-strategy;* in order to pave ways for your goals to being reached as envisioned. By this, you have to make judicious use of your subordinates, team-mates etc. to make sure you achieve your goals.

Indeed, you must not forget; that, your greatness is wrapped around your powers; which are products of your knowledge. However, your ability to polish your knowledge of choice and skills of maneuvering are what would make the world marvel at your height of greatness; unknowing you played a fast one on them, by imbibing the Columbus mentality of *deceptive-psychological-ideology*; whereby he (Columbus) deceived the world at large; even the noblest, the political chieftains, the economic moguls, including you and me to earn his marks as the chief sailor or captain that discovered *"The New Found Land"* (America) unknowing; he was as inexperienced in the sea as any novice; but because he presented himself as the best man for the job, able to convince the panel of certification of the Italian government; then got his marks alongside the gain that goes with the fame.

More so, don't always let your status mirror or reflect in your face—such as letting people read your state of mind, finance, etc in your look; instead learn to be a *chameleon-personality,* by so doing, you can charm everybody to become your admirers; by virtue of the confidence-spirit you have nurtured.

Sharpening your ego would help you chose your pattern of execution; having known what your intentions are, by so doing you had targeted at winning all to yourself and in your favour.

54

KEEP YOUR HEAD UP

Learning to take control or being in charge is a product of confidence that can project any man ahead of his counterparts in all life's endeavours. For instance, many candidates write examinations, but only the readily minded and psychological focus are those who will get the marks; and sometimes, many athletes run for a prize; it's not all that will get the crown; but only the ruthless and prepared [ones] that will carry the day—the same thing happens to kings and kingdoms; most at times, it's not the oldest or the biggest (kingdoms) but the bravest and most confidence (of himself) amongst the Kings and Queens.

Learn to be in charge, because *"If there's any royal heir in waiting; whose head fits the crown of greatness; it's you"*. All you need is become a hunter of knowledge and skills (talents) to help you build your fame and fortune (empire); that would forever reserve your crown for you; and you alone.

Moreover, try to make peace with disappointments as you borrow guide from the violent-but-calculative method of executing plans. But, you must refrain from rapacity in order to unwind the hiatus between professionalism and mediocrity.

Indeed, lend a hand from the stratagem of Napoleon Bonaparte, in that; when you are pursuing victory, you must be ruthless and when dealing with men, learn to live and see beyond them. Besides, like Selassie, you could reinforce your inner psychological tactics (tricks) involving the regal legendary of posing what you are not in order to become what you are or wannabe; because, according to Friedrich Nietzsche; ***"With all great deceivers, there's a noteworthy occurrence to which they owe their power(s) in the actual act of deception, they are overcome by belief in themselves; it's this which then speak so miraculously and compelling to those around them".*** So you could pose the best you wannabe; by deceiving every other person as far as you get your way through without ending up deceiving your own-self.

55

PLAY HIGH

The tempo of every king bearer successor or great-man's heart is usually very high, highly intense that he/she wishes to break every barriers that could militate against the realization of the intended dream(s).

Indeed, defending your charisma is the best in making your reputation stands firm and tall before your counterparts. Pay the price of maneuver in order to set the pace high and enviable. You need to play the game of a mastermind or leveraging as the case may be; whereby everyone would conclude or believe you are the real controller of the acclaimed territories in terms of finance, power or reputation. Don't forget; that was what earned Columbus his marks in 1492, with his oratory prowess, creativity and psychological doggedness by hiding his real self; but pose to the entire world that he was the highest acclaimed or known sailor (that discovered the new world [America]).

Confidence and reputation go hand-in-hand; and when one loses its stand, the other has no balance. More so, *"Reputation is like a white robe, easy to stain than remain immaculate; so beware of the companies you keep in order not to sour your reputation or lose your confidence to cowardice"*

Playing high would make you stand taller, even in the midst of the stormiest weather, due to simple secret of you knowing where you are going or what you are doing.

Mind you, don't always get too intoxicated with puffed-up spirit or self-acclaimed-super-human for the fact that you have just tasted success or greatness; besides, don't always forget; it's easier to fall than to rise. Play high, play safe, but maintain a reputable status quo, that wouldn't soil your nomenclature in the nearest or farthest future.

Reputation is a goldmine; and everyone who has it must strive to sustain it, by guarding it from the reach of (the) enemies—that's exactly why the rich see it as a taboo for them to have relationship with the have-nots in order to extend the hiatus and widen the chasm between the latter and the former. Moreover, the noblest and the richest amongst the few would wisely use their reputation to broaden their horizon.

56

WORK OUT GREATNESS

"The heights by great men reached and kept were not attained by sudden flight; but they, while their companions slept, were toiling upward in the night"—Henry Longfellow.

Throughout history, some great people had been born or identified by great traits and other successful achievements. Indeed, it's no hidden secret that, *small minds are the first to condemn great ideas*, but don't forget that it's possible because some people had seen the invisible hence their strength had become indefatigable (invincible) not because of their size, tribe or sex but because they believe they are able.

Moreover, when Charles Darwin published his first blueprint on evolution, he was faced with fierce oppositions and slanderous reproach from his fellow scientists; who where feebleminded, mediocre, agents of destruction, enemies of progress etc; all these were devised antics by the enemies to pull him down; but he kept pushing on, by means to keep his dream alive. (Darwin's Evolution)

In life, so many people had inherited greatness; some fight to take hold of it; some walk pass the corridors of greatness, while the rest cannot see the shadows of greatness. More so, some people perceive greatness, many taste greatness but in a rush; while others do not even know how it smells. For example, majority of the greatest people who had ever lived are mainly of the story of grass-to-grace i.e. starting from nobody to becoming an enviable role model to so many.

Besides, you have to take your destiny seriously; because your life is in your own hands—either you fail or succeed. Do not forget that great people had always worked extra miles and put in extra hands and brain-powers. For instance, John Pimberton (Coca-Cola) and Luigi John Baird didn't achieved their breakthroughs by mere wishes; neither did Thomas A. Edison and the Wright Brothers (Wilbur and Orville) managed to work out their greatness without focus; nor did Bill Gates and Warren Buffet fail to map-out their strategies of taking hold of the steering of fortune; but by standing against all odds despite the circle of struggles.

Do always believe in your ability, if not for anything's sake; but to paint a reliable-and-unwavering pictures of greatness; so that other people would see reasons to depend on you. For instance, if a driver seems fidgeting on the scene of an attempted accident; it will not only give the passengers doubt of his competence, but also let them lose interest in his confidence. In this, you must play the role of an experienced-but-brave driver who controls the pace of success.

Act like a pro and you will be treated as one. Don't allow your enemies and your competitors know your weaknesses—but, don't forget to hide your short comings (as a secrete that keeps you higher and going)

57

MAKE THE END MEMORABLE

It's better for the end of a thing than its genesis—Proverbs

It's the end of every action that determines who gets the glory, the money, the pride, the pedigree etc. No matter the smallness of the beginning, you must depend on the strength of your skill; so you could make a great end out of the humble beginning.

You must have a stake in whatever that transpires, either big or small; your decision must be geared towards revamping the corridors of your victory to the end. You must have eagle-vision to complement the beautiful-successful ending that comes with a humble beginning. You must polish your vision to suite your dreams; because the bible book of Proverbs. 29:18 **"Where there's no vision, the people perish";** so your vision must be vividly defined.

More so, the stakes at the end must be assured of proceeds, hopes of breakthroughs; because according to Frank Harris *"A man without ambition is like a woman without beauty".* You must keep the goals constantly in mind; by picturing the outcomes of future aspirations—such as how to get started, keep going etc. And in all, never let others (competitors etc) steal the glory or the crown it took you years to build.

Moreover, don't see obstacles as dead ends, neither must you dread them as terrors of the nights; rather fight them with all forms of seriousness and in all you have to win the battle. Indeed, Archimedes foresaw his obstacles as the threats advanced closer, he fought them with high hopes of victory; having persevered the tribulations from the government of then (the people etc), yet overcame the predicaments, from torture to slanderous abuses during the court judgements; simply because, he was seeing from his innermost mind that; ***the darkest hour is nearest the dawn;*** hence, he was perceiving the sweetness of the end beforehand; the bountifulness of the harvest would be unimaginable and at last, he took the pride by winning the crown.

The beginning might be small, do not worry, it's the end that tells the story; either sweet or sour, so, let your end ring a bell, let it sing a melodious-but-glorious song.

REFERENCES

Hornby A.S. (2001):
Oxford Learner's Advanced Dictionary.
Oxford University Press (G.B)

Mrabek, Col. James (1968):
The Art of Winning Wars
Walker & Company, New York

Niccolo Machiavelli (1940):
The Prince and the Discourses
(Translated by Luigi Ricci Christian E. Detmold)
Modern Library, New York; 1940

Richard L. Daft (2003)
Management, 6th Edition
Thompson Inc. USA

Robert Greene (2000):
The 48 Laws of Power
Penguin Books Ltd, USA

Webster's Comprehensive Dictionary.
Deluxe Encyclopedia Edition
Typhoon International Corporation
U.S.A. 2004

Wilfred D. Best (2001):
The Students' Companion Revised Edition.
Longman Press